How to talk to anyone, the essential keys to better communication and dialogue

Patience John

TABLE OF CONTENT

PREFACE

Who is this book for?

This book is designed for individuals who face challenges when it comes to engaging in quality conversations. It is intended for those who aspire to excel in their everyday interactions with people and wish to use their words effectively to make a positive impact on others. Understanding how to communicate in a manner that resonates well with listeners is a key focus of this book.

Additionally, this book is beneficial for romantic partners who struggle with maintaining healthy communication in their relationships. It offers insights and strategies to improve dialogue and connection. Similarly, parents who find it difficult to communicate with their teenagers or young adults will discover valuable lessons within these pages to better understand and support their children.

However, this book is not limited to specific groups mentioned above—it is relevant to everyone who engages in interpersonal communication, which is a fundamental aspect of our lives. Effective communication skills are essential for building relationships, fostering understanding, and achieving personal and professional success. Therefore, whether you are seeking to enhance your conversations at work, with friends, family, or in romantic relationships, this book offers practical guidance and techniques to elevate your communication abilities and enrich your interactions.

How this book should be use

This book is a comprehensive guide to effective communication, providing you with everything you need to know. Treat it as your go-to resource for practical tips that you can quickly reference wherever you are. Its compact size makes it convenient to carry along, ensuring you have access to valuable insights whenever you need them.

For optimal enjoyment, consider reading this book during moments of relaxation or during your personal "me" time. Keep it neatly stored on a bookshelf or table to maintain a clutter-free home or office space. This way, you can easily access its wealth of knowledge whenever you're ready to enhance your communication skills.

INTRODUCTION

Have you ever said something and immediately regretted it, thinking, "Oh no, that didn't come out right"? Many of us have experienced this, including myself before I embarked on my journey as a relationship therapist. I've since helped thousands of people online and offline to improve their relationships using various tools, and I can tell you that communication is absolutely essential in this endeavour.

Let me address a common issue among those who are knowledgeable or tend to talk a lot, which I too have struggled with in the past. When someone is well-informed, they may struggle with effective communication. Communication isn't just about talking—it's about listening and giving others the chance to express themselves too.

Those who always have something to say may overlook the importance of allowing others to contribute to the conversation. This was a hurdle I faced after spending 12 years earning my degrees in psychology, including a BSc, Masters, and PhD, followed by six years studying relationship therapy at Stanford University and the University of Colorado. With all this knowledge, I believed I had answers to every question and problem, typical of a therapist.

However, my extensive knowledge affected my communication skills. I realized that effective communication requires more than just knowledge; it demands self-discipline and empathy. Without these qualities, conversations become one-sided, lacking impact or connection.

Imagine talking more than listening when someone seeks your guidance. They may become disengaged, leading to ineffective communication and unmet needs. I encountered this challenge first-hand with my first client, Tracy, in El Centro, California. Despite knowing what she needed, I found myself talking instead of truly communicating, doing 76% of the talking.

To improve, I delved into personal development and self-discipline, transforming my communication skills in just a few months. This shift enabled me to connect authentically and effectively with others.

Why should you consider learning these skills? Communication impacts lives profoundly. A good communicator doesn't just talk—they convey meaning and understanding. By mastering communication, you'll discern others' needs and perspectives, guiding conversations toward constructive outcomes.

This book equips you with essential communication tools. Each chapter blends theory with practical strategies for effective dialogue. Whether you're seeking personal growth or professional development, mastering these skills will elevate your ability to connect and communicate effectively in every aspect of life.

CHAPTER ONE
What you should know about effective communication

Effective communication is about more than just sharing ideas. It's about getting the emotion and intentions behind the material. As well as being able to clearly express a message, you need to also listen in a way that gets the full meaning of what's being said and makes the other person feel heard and understood.

Effective conversation sounds like it should be intuitive. But all too often, when we try to connect with others something goes wrong. We say one thing, the other person hears something else, and misunderstandings, anger, and conflicts follow. This can cause problems in your home, school, and work ties.

For many of us, speaking more clearly and successfully means learning some important skills. Whether you're trying to improve communication with your spouse, kids, boss, or coworkers, learning these skills can strengthen your ties to others, build greater trust and respect, and improve teamwork, problem solving, and your general social and mental health. Therefore to become effective in communication there are skills you need to have, and one of those skills we will be discussing, is Empathy.

Empathy in Communication

Being empathetic means being able to understand and feel what someone else is feeling. If you put yourself in someone else's shoes, you might be more likely to care about them and do what you can to make their situation better and when that is the case you will be able to communicate exactly what the person needs to hear at such time and you can ease your own and the other person's stress by doing this.

For example, when you get home, you find out that your partner or husband is sick. You would feel their pain and take care of their needs even if your day was going smoothly. Of course, you'd feel the same way if a friend was mad at their boss for how they treated them. You might not be able to solve their problem, but you can see why they need to let off steam.

Empathy isn't just for dealing with bad things. You can feel your child's happiness when they are happy about something. If your friend is laughing at a joke, you can feel their happiness. Empathy helps you to deepen your connections as you connect with friends' and loved ones' thoughts and feelings, and they connect with yours.

Empathy can stretch to people you don't know as well. If you saw someone sitting alone at a party, for example, you might connect with their loneliness and chat with them. If you saw pictures of other people suffering on the other side of the world, you might be moved to give resources to help ease their suffering. On the other hand, when you see a broadcast crowd roaring with joy, you might feel your feelings rise. Their delight becomes your pleasure. That's the power of empathy and having empathy will boost the quality and effectiveness of your communication because you will communicate base on their situation and your message will be received well not just because you want to say something.

Especially to a very close person to you, either a spouse, family member or a friend, empathy will help you communicate better and reach the heart.

Speaking with Empathy

Listen Actively: When someone speaks to you, pay complete attention. Maintain eye contact, nod periodically, and don't interrupt. Demonstrate that you are truly interested in what they have to say.

Acknowledge Feelings: Try to identify and acknowledge the feelings that the other person is feeling. You can say something like, "It sounds like you're frustrated" or "I can understand why that would make you excited."

Use Open-Ended Questions: Rather of asking yes/no questions, use open-ended inquiries that invite the other person to reveal more about their thoughts and feelings. Like the question, "How did that make you feel?" or "Can you tell me more about what happened?"

Validate Their Experience: Demonstrate comprehension by confirming their experience. You may respond by saying, "It makes sense that you would feel that way" rather than "I understand why you're upset about this."

Reflect Back: Summarise what the other person has stated to demonstrate that you have listened and clarified your comprehension. "So, if I understand correctly, you're saying…" This ensures you're on the same page.

Offer Support: Demonstrate that you're there to assist or support in any manner you can. Ask the question, "What can I do to help?" "Is there anything you need from me?"

Be Genuine: Authenticity is essential while communicating with empathy. Mean what you say and allow your compassion to shine through organically.

Pay Attention To Your Tone: Be mindful of your tone of speech and body language. A warm and compassionate tone is more effective for conveying empathy.

Avoid Judgement: Do not criticise or judge the other person's feelings or experiences. Every viewpoint is legitimate.

CHAPTER TWO
Listening

You can't fully communicate without listening, and your communication skills aren't complete if you don't know how to listen. As we discussed, empathy helps you understand the other person's immediate needs, enabling you to communicate in a way that truly benefits or resonates with them. However, listening is essential for developing empathy.

If you don't want to hear what someone has to say, you can't put yourself in their place. That's why being able to listen well is so important for communicating effectively. It's not enough to just act like you're listening. Try to pay close attention so that you can understand the other person's thoughts, feelings, and situation.

Find and get rid of things that make it hard to listen. It will be tough to pay attention to the other person if you're feeling stressed. If something is causing you worry, like a deadline or a toothache, you might want to deal with it before continuing the talk. Multitasking is another common thing that gets in the way of careful listening. Stop what you're doing and put down your phone so you can give the other person your full attention. This is particularly important during disagreements or when broaching sensitive or complex topics.

Do not interrupt. When you cut people off, you not only stop their train of thought but you also risk misunderstanding the point they were trying to make. In addition, if you're formulating your next line while the other person is still talking, you're not totally listening and your reply may not be what you should have said and what resonate with their needs.

Withhold judgment. If you know you disagree with someone, you might find yourself thinking undermining their words as they speak. But it's best to listen with an open mind. Don't quickly criticize or place blame while they're talking. Make a real effort to understand where they're coming from.

Let the other person know you're listening. Non-verbal cues, such as keeping eye contact, a head nod, and vocal cues, such as a quick "uh-huh," let the other person know they have your attention. You're basically asking them to continue. If you appear to be daydreaming or thinking about something else, the speaker might take that as a sign that you don't care.

This practical skill is highly beneficial when communicating with your spouse, family, or friends. They will sense first-hand that you genuinely care about them and have their best interests at heart.

If you are a friend to someone equipped with effective communication tools such as empathy and active listening, they are more likely to seek your advice or confide in you because they trust you to provide thoughtful responses. In the next chapter, we will delve deeper into the various aspects of listening and how you can better understand others.

5 barrier to listening

Knowing these barriers will help you know if you really need to work on yourself extremely and improve on your listening skills or you are doing well already in that aspect.

Distractions: External distractions such as noise or visible information can make it difficult to focus on the person you are talking to.

Prejudice or Bias: Preconceived ideas or biases about the person or to you can prevent you or them to be active and open their mind to listen.

Lack of Empathy: Failing to connect with the person you are trying to communicate with their feelings or experiences can lead to mistakes and miscommunication just we discussed earlier

Interrupting or Over-talking: When you try dominate the conversation, it can impede your ability to deliver your message.

Personal Concerns: Being preoccupied with personal problems or thoughts can prevent you from active and careful listening.

CHAPTER THREE
Read body language

Listening isn't just about getting verbal words. People also communicate information about their mental state through nonverbal body cues. The skill to read body language is useful in all kinds of social situations and interaction

Perhaps you have a friend who frequently says, "I'm doing OK," but you can tell by their gloomy face that something is wrong. Or maybe you can judge a date's interest in you based on their amount of eye contact.

People often send ideas through:

Facial attitude. Frowns, grins, uncertain smiles, and other facial expressions can communicate mood.

Eye contact. A person's eyes might be aimed at whatever they're focused on. Wide eyes can express joy. Drooping lids might imply that the person is tired or calm.

Voice. A person's speaking tone can tell you if they're playing or being serious. The speed at which they talk can express confidence or nervousness.

Posture. Stiff, tight shoulders might indicate anxiety. Relaxed shoulders and a slouching stance might be a sign that the person is at ease or bored.

Gestures. Lack of hand movements may suggest shyness or discomfort. Someone who's feeling free and friendly might use their hands more. The speed and intensity of the movements can also express anger or excitement.

Reading body language can be hard. Not everyone uses the exact same visual cues. And certain cues can mean various things. For example, is a person tapping their finger on the table because they're feeling impatient or because they're liking the song playing in the background? Here's what to consider when trying to understand someone's body language:

Look for stability. Nonverbal cues should match what the other person is saying. If your partner says they're nervous, their pacing or furrowed face might support this message. In cases where body language doesn't match what's being said, you might need to make more of an effort to understand how the other person is feeling.

Don't read too much into individual signs. If you focus too much on any one sign, you're likely to misunderstand the other person. For example, just because a person is looking away from you doesn't mean they're uninterested. They might simply be gathering their thoughts. When reading body language, look at multiple cues to gain a more complete idea. In the nutshell when all these effective communication tools are used you are more likely to know what to say or what not to say to a person and also to help them to open up and communicate to you, by then there will be a proper and effective communication

Being aware of your own body language

Remember that your behavioural cues are also sending messages to people around you. If you're sitting with your arms crossed and looking away from the other person, they might take that as a sign that you don't want to talk.

For example, if you want to encourage your romantic partner to connect with you, use positive signs, such as a gentle smile and relaxed eye contact, to project love. Learning ways to handle stress can help you avoid unconscious negative cues, such as frowning and keeping a rigid stance.

The truth is, you can't have an effective communication if your body language isn't giving your listener the idea that you are listening to them – so while you bend on studying the other person's body language, don't forget to keep yours in check.

CHAPTER FOUR

How to express yourself when you are angry

When you're angry, a lot can go wrong. You might damage relationships, hurt someone's feelings deeply, or say things that are hard to take back. For instance, imagine having a heated argument with your partner, and they suddenly say, "I never loved you and only married you for your money." Such hurtful words can shatter trust and leave lasting wounds in a relationship.

That's why it's crucial to learn how to express yourself effectively when you're angry. By preparing in advance, you can avoid causing irreparable harm in the heat of the moment..

When you're feeling angry, it's important to express yourself in a way that communicates your feelings without causing harm. Let us take a look on how you should do this.

1. Take a Breath

Before saying anything, take a deep breath to calm yourself down. This simple action can help you think more clearly and prevent you from saying something you might regret later.

2. Identify Your Feelings

Try to pinpoint exactly what is making you angry. Is it something specific that someone said or did? Understanding your feelings can help you express yourself more effectively.

3. Use "I" Statements:

Instead of blaming others, use sentences that start with "I feel" to express your emotions. For example, say "I feel upset when this happens" rather than "You always make me mad."

4. Be Assertive, Not Aggressive:

It's okay to assert your feelings, but avoid being aggressive or confrontational. Speak in a calm and respectful tone, even if you're upset.

5. Listen to the Other Person

Allow the other person to share their perspective without interrupting. This shows that you respect their point of view and can lead to a more productive conversation.

6. Focus on Solutions:

Instead of dwelling on what went wrong, focus on finding a solution together. This can help diffuse tension and prevent the situation from escalating.

7. Take a Break if Needed:

 If you feel too overwhelmed or the conversation becomes too heated, it's okay to take a break. You can always revisit the discussion when you're both feeling calmer.

8. Seek Understanding, Not Just Agreement

Sometimes, the goal isn't to make the other person agree with you but to ensure they understand your feelings. Mutual understanding can often lead to better outcomes.

9. Use Positive Body Language

 Your body language can also convey your emotions. Try to maintain open and relaxed posture, avoid crossing your arms, and make eye contact to show that you're engaged.

Remember, expressing anger is natural, but how you express it can make a big difference in resolving conflicts positively. By communicating your feelings effectively and respectfully, you can strengthen your relationships with people and find healthier ways to manage your emotions.

CHAPTER FIVE

How the three A's can help – Applaud, Appreciation, and Admire.

When we talk about good conversation, it's not just what we say; it's also about how we make other people feel. This is where giving praise, thanks, and admiration come in they're like the secret sauce that makes conversation important and strong.

Is easier to overlook some of the aspect of communication that has to do with cheering others up and making them feel good within themselves.

In this chapter we will consider the three A's in connection to an effective communication. Let start with

Applaud

First, let's talk about applauding. When we praise someone during a talk, it's like giving them a virtual pat on the back. It shows that we respect their thoughts, efforts, or achievements. This simple act can improve their confidence and create a happy atmosphere. For instance, if a partner suggests a great idea in a meeting, acknowledging it with applause can drive them and encourage more useful contributions. In your conversation

Appreciation

Next, Appreciation is a game-changer in conversation. When we appreciate someone, we show gratitude or recognize their traits. Saying "thank you" truly or acknowledging someone's hard work not only makes them feel good but also improves the bond between people. For instance, if a friend helps you out with a project, showing real thanks can strengthen your bond and encourage future cooperation.

Admire

Admiration adds a special touch to conversation. When we admire someone, we show our respect or awe for their qualities or successes. Sharing praise can motivate others and build a sense of connection. For example, if you admire a colleague's innovative approach to problem-solving, letting them know can inspire them to keep pushing limits.

Combining applaud, appreciation, and admiration makes our conversation deeper and more effective. It promotes positivity, builds relationships, and supports a supportive atmosphere. So, the next time you interact, remember the power of these simple yet powerful actions. They can turn an everyday exchange into something truly special!

Let's see how you can best practice these essential tools with a workmate, friend, family member, and spouse.

How to apply the three A's when communicating with a workmate, Friend, Family member, and spouse

Workmate

Applaud: In a work setting, applaud your workmate's achievements or contributions during team meetings. For example, say, "Great job on that presentation, it was very well done!"

Appreciate: Show appreciation for their efforts by thanking them for their hard work or assistance on a project. For instance, say, "Thank you for your help with the report; your insights were invaluable."

Admire: Express admiration for their skills or expertise. For example, say, "I really admire how you handle challenging tasks with such calmness and efficiency."

Friend

Applaud: Celebrate your friend's successes or milestones. For instance, say, "Congratulations on landing that new job! You deserve it."

Appreciate: Show appreciation for their friendship and support. For example, say, "I appreciate how you're always there for me when I need someone to talk to."

Admire: Express admiration for their unique qualities or achievements. For example, say, "I admire your adventurous spirit; you always inspire me to try new things."

Family Member

Applaud: Applaud family members for their accomplishments or personal growth. For example, say, "I'm proud of you for sticking to your fitness routine; you've come a long way!"

Appreciate: Express gratitude for their love and care. For instance, say, "I appreciate everything you do for our family; you're the backbone of our household."

Admire: Share admiration for their resilience or positive traits. For example, say, "I admire how you stay so optimistic even during tough times."

Spouse

Applaud: Celebrate your spouse's achievements and successes. For instance, say, "I'm so proud of how hard you've been working. Your dedication is inspiring."

Appreciate: Show appreciation for their presence and support in your life. For example, say, "I appreciate you for always being my rock and supporting me through thick and thin."

Admire: Express admiration for their character or qualities that you love. For example, say, "I admire your kindness and generosity; it's what drew me to you in the first place."

In summary, incorporating applaud, appreciation, and admiration into conversations with different people shows that you value and respect them. These gestures can strengthen bonds and foster a positive and supportive environment in both personal and professional relationships.

Practicing Communication to Perfection

Effective conversation is a skill that can be honed through careful practice and mindful application. To truly excel in conversation, take these steps:

Self-Awareness: Understand your communication style, skills, and places for growth. Reflect on past encounters to spot trends and learn from mistakes.

Active Listening: Practice active listening by giving full attention to the speaker, showing understanding, and asking clarifying questions. This helps in getting others' perspectives and responding properly.

Clarity and Conciseness: Work on communicating thoughts clearly and concisely. Avoid jargon or overly complicated wording, and focus on presenting your point in a straightforward way.

Body Language: Pay attention to your body language, as it can greatly impact how your message is received. Maintain eye contact, use open movements, and be aware of your stance.

Empathy and Emotional Intelligence: Develop empathy to connect with others on an emotional level. Understand and control your own emotions while being sensitive to the feelings of others.

Practice Active Engagement: Engage in regular talks with various people to build confidence and adaptability in communication. Seek comments to improve and polish your skills.

Adaptability: Learn to adapt your speaking style based on the scenario and audience. Tailor your message to be more successful and approachable.

Continuous Improvement: Treat conversation as an ongoing process of growth. Seek chances to learn from experts, attend classes, or read books on effective speaking.

By adding these practices into your daily conversations, you can improve your communication skills and become a more confident and persuasive communicator

CHAPTER SIX

How Listening, speaking with clarity, and understanding can help achieve effective communication

Achieving effective communication involves a combination of active listening, speaking with clarity, and demonstrating understanding. These elements are crucial in fostering clear and meaningful interactions in both personal and professional settings. Let's explore how each component contributes to effective communication:

Listening with Intent

Listening is the foundation of effective communication. When you listen actively and with intent, you demonstrate genuine interest in the speaker and their message. Here's how listening enhances communication:

Builds Trust and Rapport: Actively listening shows respect and empathy, which helps build trust and rapport with the speaker.

Enhances Understanding: Listening attentively allows you to grasp the speaker's thoughts, feelings, and perspectives accurately.

Minimizes Misunderstandings: By listening carefully, you can clarify any points of confusion or ambiguity, reducing the risk of miscommunication.

Speaking with Clarity

Speaking clearly is essential for conveying your message effectively. When you communicate with clarity, you make it easier for others to understand and respond appropriately. Here's why speaking clearly is important:

Conveys Message Effectively: Clear communication ensures that your message is conveyed accurately and comprehensively.

Engages the Audience or individual: Clear speech captures the listener's attention and keeps them focused on the content being communicated.

Reduces Misinterpretation: Speaking clearly minimizes the risk of misunderstandings or misinterpretations, leading to smoother interactions.

Demonstrating Understanding

Demonstrating understanding involves showing empathy and acknowledging the speaker's viewpoint. It is an integral part of effective communication that fosters mutual respect and cooperation. Here's how understanding contributes to effective communication:

Promotes Empathy: Acknowledging the speaker's feelings and perspectives demonstrates empathy and validates their experiences.

Encourages Openness: When you show understanding, it encourages open and honest communication, creating a supportive environment.

Facilitates Problem-Solving: Understanding the speaker's point of view allows for constructive dialogue and collaborative problem-solving.

Combining These Elements

When you integrate active listening, speaking with clarity, and demonstrating understanding into your communication approach, you can achieve the following benefits:

Improved Relationships Effective communication strengthens relationships by fostering trust, empathy, and mutual respect.

Enhanced Collaboration: Clear communication promotes teamwork and collaboration, leading to better outcomes in group settings.

Conflict Resolution: Understanding each other's perspectives and communicating clearly can help resolve conflicts peacefully and constructively.

Increased Productivity: Effective communication reduces misunderstandings and enhances efficiency in task completion and goal achievement.

To summarise, mastering the art of listening, speaking with clarity, and demonstrating understanding is essential for achieving effective communication. These skills not only facilitate better interactions but also contribute to building strong relationships, fostering collaboration, and achieving shared objectives in various aspects of life. Practice and hone these skills to become a more proficient communicator and enjoy the benefits of clearer, more meaningful connections with others.

CONCLUSION

In conclusion, communication is the lifeline that connects us to others, enriches our relationships, and drives positive outcomes in both personal and professional areas. As we navigate the art of effective communication, there are key factors to always keep in mind:

Firstly, never underestimate the power of listening with understanding and speaking with clarity. Genuine understanding promotes trust and mutual respect, paving the way for meaningful connections.

Secondly, know that effective communication is not just about transmitting information; it's about eliciting understanding and alignment. Clear, concise, and considerate communication can resolve conflicts, inspire action, and support cooperation.

Lastly, continue to apply and refine your communication skills because they are important for success in every aspect of life. Whether you're nurturing relationships, navigating challenges, or chasing goals, effective communication will be your greatest asset.

Ultimately, effective communication is vital because it cultivates harmony, promotes efficiency, and enables personal growth. By honing these skills and staying committed to continuous growth, you'll not only enhance your interactions but also enrich your life and the lives of those around you. Keep practicing, keep learning, and keep communicating—it's the key to unlocking boundless possibilities and meaningful connections in the world.

BONUS
Communicating in Different Settings: What to say

Have you ever found yourself avoiding someone because you weren't sure what to say to them, especially during their best or worst moments? Maybe you've tried to offer words of comfort or congratulations, but ended up feeling like your message came across as awkward or conveyed a different meaning than intended. Knowing what to say in sensitive situations requires empathy, compassion, and tact. Here are thoughtful responses for various life events:

Loss of a Loved One

"I'm deeply sorry for your loss. Please know that I will always reach out to you and offer support and I will have you in my prayers for you to heal in time'

Going Through a Break-Up

"I'm here to support you during this difficult time. Take it one day at a time, and remember that you're not alone, you will be blessed with someone better"

Losing a Job

"I'm sorry to hear about your job. I believe in your skills and resilience. Let me know how I can assist you during this transition."

Miscarriage

"I'm so sorry for your loss. Take the time you need to heal, and know that I'm here just as your wonderful family members and good friends are here to cheer you up and help you cope for a better time"

Natural Disaster

" I really understand and feel the pain of losing everything, is devastating but I believe that life is precious too and I'm relieved to hear that you're safe, you will always get there again. If there's anything you need, please don't hesitate to reach out."

Illness

"Wishing you a speedy recovery. Let me know if there's anything I can do to help make this time easier for you."

Achievement

"Congratulations on your remarkable achievement! You've worked hard for this and deserve every bit of success. I wish you more wins in the future"

Good Grades

"Well done on your excellent grades! Your dedication and effort are truly commendable."

Marriage

"Congratulations on your marriage! Wishing you a lifetime of happiness and love together."

Birth of a Child

"Congratulations on the arrival of your baby! What wonderful news! Wishing you joy and precious moments with your little one."

Graduation

"Congratulations on your graduation! Your hard work has paid off, and I'm excited to see where your journey takes you next."

Admission to a Program

"Congratulations on your admission! This is a testament to your capabilities and potential."

Recovery from Illness

"I'm thrilled to hear that you're feeling better. Take care and continue to prioritize your health."

Escape from Danger

"I'm so relieved to know you're safe. Let me know if there's anything you need."

Shared Problem/Challenge

"We're in this together. I'm here to help and support you through this."

Communicate Right.

communicate with anyone.

UNLOCKING THE SECRETS TO GAINING
MASS!
10
Steps
CLASSIFIED
TO ACHIEVING
YOUR DREAM SIZE!